Korban Quest

Poems by Neil Spirtas

Wider Perspectives Publishing, Norfolk, Va. 2023, 2nd ed.

Other books by the author:

Florida's Forgotten Crackers
When Men Cry: Life's Later Voyages

Cover Art:
"Bridge Above the Mighty Waters"
Photograph by Neil H. Spirtas

To my wife Robyn, mentor Dr. C. David Anderson
and parents Irv and Gert Spirtas - of blessed memory,
my poetry friends Benjamin Hyland, M.B. McLatchey,
Mary Anderson Read, and Reb Tuviah Schreiber.

Table of Contents

Introduction

Author's Notes

About the Author

Introduction

Korban Quest is a spiritual, "drawing closer" endeavor. The book navigates between friends, family, a culture and a tradition, the natural world and the spiritual one.

The Hebrew word *Korban* comes originally from the commandments in the Torah for sacrificial offerings. Doing homage in ancient times required great offerings, but after the catastrophic events surrounding the destruction of the Second Temple in 70 CE, Jews turned to prayer for atonement (instead of sacrifices) and "to reach out" and draw closer to G-d.

Poet Laureate of Volusia County, Florida M.B. McLatchey says, "it takes a *good* person to be a good poet and she tries to emulate in her work – empathy, authenticity, and self-effacement". Her mentor Poet Seamus Heaney, and 1995 Nobel Prize winner in Literature, described this *goodness* as something he strived for; "a positioning in service to the world".

In Judaism, the term to describe Heaney's "positioning" is referred to as Tikkun Olam. To do good in the world, to strive for "saving the world" by good deeds is an inherent responsibility we all share with one another.

Norma L. Goodrich in her Afterword to the book, **The Man Who Wanted Trees** (by Jean Giono) said that "hopefulness must spring from literature and the profession of poetry". The poet's mission "is to remind us of beauty, of trees swaying in the breeze, or pines groaning under snow in the mountain passes, of wild white horses galloping across the surf."

It is our responsibility, as writers, to profess being good and sweet faithfulness – in the magic and mystery of our words.

My hope is readers will find your own *Korban* journey as fruitful and phenomenal as mine.

Neil Spirtas

Would I Have Survived

in this *land on the edge*?

Would I have survived
for being a *Tzadik* and writing on the fringe?

Would I have been imprisoned
for speaking out about community?

Would I have been assassinated
for freedom and free thinking?

Wouldn't militarily muscle and might,
continue to dash the dreams and right ...

of this and many a writer and poet?

Would displaced Jews have been impoverished
to lives no one chooses?

Would the greater society suffer?
All the while, a stifled Ukrainian voice loses.

When one person was liberated,
then the whole world was saved.

Would I have survived,
while hidden potential was within my grip?

When earthly peace and justice
would have flowed

from *Elijah's* cup for all to sip.

Could a Hitler Rise Again?

"Do not stand idly by when your brother's life is in danger."
- Leviticus

Today mental illnesses are increasing,
with new terminology coined for classifying
suicides by our juveniles and the young.
Fear and terrorism are so insane.

Could a Hitler rise again!?

Not as easily defined is charisma,
endeared by the good, the bad, the indifferent.
Beware of this slippery dogma,
catapulting leaders to reign.

Could a Hitler really come again?

Has our humankind come so far in fear,
within a century,
to turn its head from
violence, pain, suffering, and misery?

Are the righteous so few and far between,
to allow a Hitler upon the scene?
In the name of so-called justice and equality,

in these *nations of strangers, bowling and living alone,*
who would atone?
For all the societal vice and vain,

Could a Hitler rise again!?

What Being a Jew Means

An inquiring Yiddish phrase
and quest to provoke our young and old.

What being a Jew means
more than our stories have told.

More than attending Hebrew school, a Bar Mitzvah,
and definitions on maternal lineage; ages old.

More than latkes and kugels or a bialy
with a schmear of cream cheese and lox,

Jewish High Holidays with friends and family,
gravesite visits honoring the dead with headstone rocks.

A constant query and responsibility
into the meaning of being Jewish

and choices of right and wrong.
A compassionate culture and tradition

of ritual and song.
Talmudic teachings thousands of centuries' long.

What being a Jew means
is more than secular survival.

But *L'dor Vador:*
A disciplining not of force nor only of reason

but of a Bible profound in faith and belief
for a greater good and civilization.

If age today has conventionally replaced
classical natural wisdom,

then one of the oldest and wisest of them all
would be Judaism.

What being a Jew means to me,
even though nothing is comparable,

is striving to be G-d-like, in the image of, and for
aspiring Jews and Gentiles alike.

On Faith

"For my sake the world was created." - Talmud
"I am but dust and ashes." - Genesis

For your sake, the earth was made
redeemed from burnt offerings.
Yet to whom do you love,

to whom do you believe in,
to whom do you worship,
who created your world?

Take back *Satan*, the adversary, the wanderer.
Take but for the people, like a Leviathan in their minds,
whom relish in their insanity.

Be faithful to your G-d,
be fruitful, counsel with the angels,
be humble; for there is no one else.

Through deeds of redemption in your *Nefesh*:
You may now love, praising more than sacrificing.
You should honor the hovering upon the face of the waters.

The promise of a great nation
to see but a facsimile of a burning bush:
To see the face of G-d.

Love Inspires

us to shape our world,
to ignite the spark in others.

Love may not feed the hungry,
nor cement a broken bone.

Nor save us from tsunamis,
nor bring back the concentration camp victims.

But love can help you look at yourself
reflect at the river's edge,

see most clearly on a mountaintop,
lead our country on the field of battle.

Heal a wounded soldier's sorrow,
bring *tzedakah* to loved ones.

Love inspires us to
rise higher than yourself alone.

Rifka's Mezuzah

My friend Rifka's *mezuzah* was
sewed and secretly saved by her mother
from the Nazis,
just inside the bosom,
inner lining of her coat.
The *mezuzah* was hidden asunder
by her mother -
unbeknownst to Rifka.
For all they had in their possession,
on the way to Bergen-Belsen,
was a knapsack with the bare essentials -
a towel, a change of clothes, and
a toothbrush.
The *mezuzah*, the length of one's hand,
contained only the parchment.
The casing was left behind.
A most honored motherly gift on Rifka's wedding day
to help remember the days of Moses.
When the Jews were passed over
by the Angel of Death.
Not a superstition, nor a good luck charm.
L'dor Vador, the *Shema*, and much more,
is what it was written for:
For the plea,
for the only deity,
for the Almighty to protect
their coming in and their going out,
for all eternity.

Checked Your Mezuzah Lately?

Have you *checked your mezuzah* lately?
Has the scroll's ink smudged beyond readability?
Just perhaps your life

has taken a sullen path –
you've lost your way,
your job, your wife.

In reverence do we kiss,
not unlike the woman of valor,
keeping the words of the *mezuzah* on our lips.

Humbly we enter the comforts of one's home,
one's doorpost,
one's gates.

Reading the words on skin of animal parchment,
its ink infused from vegetables.
Savor this ancient, blessed treasure

at a thirty percent angle,
in a permanent place,
so many will embrace.

Perhaps Rifka's *teshuva* journey was
to return rather reluctantly
to a time to pass from her,

to her daughter,
to her granddaughter,
to a place on the doorpost of their house.

Where they spend most of their days
to heal others, to help all,
to be a *light unto the nations*.

The Shema: A Watchword Prayer

"If you pray only according to the precise text in the siddur
and nothing from your heart your prayer is not complete." - Talmud

At least twice a day one should say -
With all your heart, with all your might,
with all your soul.

Even in times of peril
under the evil Roman empire,
under the pharaohs and idols before you,

under the doorposts of your house and upon your gate.
Hear, oh descendants of Israel:
Listen, listen, pay attention.

Focus, focus, people of G-d's imagination
in crossing the Jordan to the promised land.
There is no way to explain,

there is only to elevate,
there is but to contemplate,
there is no one else - *Ein od, Ein od.*

But to love, when we breath in,
when we rise up, and
when we lie down.

The Old Country

Deprived of the records on family history
and past hardships,
I envision how my ancestors escaped
the camps and dictatorships.
I traversed the Old Country
along the stately Dnieper's gates
and tributaries.
Life and the land have changed
by its inhabitants and boundaries.
How many were killed
in the streets, in the camps,
in the ravines,
of Odessa and Babi Yar?
Persecuted, ridiculed, condemned:
I know not their names.
Their bodies desecrated:
Their humanity not entirely living.
To those righteous gentiles –
to the Jewish saviors,
I give blessing
for your family and lives
left behind.
Rows and rows of crumbling sandstone,
remnants of WW II's destruction
of Stalin's and Putin's kind.
G-d grant this nation –
melancholic,
beautiful,
historic,
rich land of contradiction,
a Renaissance of hope.

Seahorse Stables Shabbat

Riding horseback on the sandy beaches
and whitecapped waters,
overlooking the Atlantic's sapphire blue waves,
with gusts of sun-sifted wind currents
swirling at my back.

Tranquilly, the horse and I
are now one.
We breath in and out
of the mouth of nature's universe:
The sweet spot of this elegant and loyal animal.

Retiring to the shackles of his stall
from the saddle of many a brazen rider.
Finally free and at rest,
for now,
from the weight of the world off his back.

We have been on such a narrow path.
Traversing the back breaking miles
he has carried us because that is what he does.
Until returning home then he starts all over again –
the journey of the next rider.

But does he really come home to rest on *shabbat* with the other horses?
Unlike a bareback balancing trek with us holding his mane.
'Tis much better than a rein.
To trade in
to a kinder, gentler
fiddler on the roof

Remember the traditions specially to *keep the Sabbath holy:*
For your sons, your daughters, your cattle, your horses,
even the strangers in the settlements.
So, they too
may rest – as do you.

Hanukkah of Old

Eight days we revel about *the miracle of oil.*
We light candles to shine brightly on every 25th of Kislev.
A miracle they lasted way beyond
when they were supposed to run their course.

Rededicating Hanukkah of Old
for the Temple 2000 years ago.
Celebrating *Teshuva* for a new home.
Rebuilding and reclaiming Israel for the Jewish nation.

A *mezuzah* hangs on this doorpost, along with a
menorah of bold, brilliant, brass.
Euphoric were the Maccabees
with their newfound oil fried delicacies and latkes.

My time now to praise our ancestors
forced into the pogroms of the potato fields:
Fermenting potatoes in a distillery of alcohol.
Founding our family name

from which they made their livelihood,
from which only a few occupations existed.

My Soul

"If l am not for myself, who will be for me and if l am only for myself what am I, and if not now, when?" - Hillel wisdom

It is my soul awakening,
my soul speaking.
It is my memories,
my soul alive and listening.
It is the rapid fire of
questions and answers,
isolated,
by an alias of
my own Socratic method.
Rippling through me,
my *nefesh* in mid-air,
the breath created
out of thin air.
Converging with torrents
of wisdom nearby,
patiently pending with other souls,
breathing on the banks below.
Then evolving into the
Burning Palace.
It is me conversing, wrestling in the universe
with G-d.
It is from dust to discourse with the heavenly bodies.
It is about what I've shared and given away,
but it is not all about me.

The Jewish Way

Magnificent history and record-keepers,
storytelling antiquity and Talmudic thinkers,
debaters, teachers, and Socratic dialogue users,
protectors of the human condition and of creation.
Molders of a language and culture,
through a mindful *sechel*,
courageously from Africa to the Far East.
Leaders and *people of the book* –
from Abraham, Isaac, and Jacob
Sarah, Rebecca, Rachel, and Leah to
Moses and Maimonides.
Survivors of extreme intolerances,
surpassing the greatest of Greek plays.
Weaving a bold, proud fabric,
symbolic as the skullcap or the Star of David –
The Jewish Way.

A way of life, an eternal philosophy,
a contemplative, ancient tradition.
Both Ashkenazi and Sephardic: Brutally tragic.
Bifurcating families beyond recognition:
But never again!

Sentimental rhythms of song at shul
and melodic qualities recalling our youth.
Weave a spell and mood that
tantalizes the senses, fills the air, removes the pain.
Peaceful, incredible breathes after a summer rain.

Bitter herbs and sweet sorrows pass over the generations.
Charoset hardening the foundations for the anointed world to come.
Free now, never forgetting albeit forgiving,
praying, bypassing a stultifying, lamenting past.
Jettisoned to another world to come at long last.
Tears well up like the steam
on the mirror from a hot shower,
kvelling over a mother's child's accomplishments –
The Jewish Way.

Misunderstood

"It is not for you to complete the task, but neither are you free to stand aside from it." - Mishnah Sage, Rabbi Tarfon

How and when did Job's patience become a truism?
A conflicted, misunderstood maxim?
Do people get what is coming to them?
Have life's obstacles overwhelmed them?
Has their vision, their dreams become clouded?
Has a once fervent faith become flawed like *smoked vapor*?

Take in the far-reaching teachings of the *Talmud*.
Study the *Torah* on your bookshelf library, not in Heaven.
You say the Old Testament is decrepit, a relic:
Regard them both with a sense of awe, of wonder.

Hear, hear their great mysteries.
In times of great mourning
we turn our heads to the Heavens,
to our relationships to gain strength,
to pray the Mourner's Kaddish – with no word in it of death:
Even at our doorsteps and in our house.

Considered chosen by G-d,
for what, for special treatment,
for a favorite son,
for being better than anyone else?

No, no,
we have a special job to do:
Our people have been let go …
to serve, to worship in the wilderness*.
To bring *Torah* into the world,
to be a light unto the nations.

To be people of the book.
Even while our books have been burnt,
even while we are so small in numbers,
even while we have the most hate crimes against.

Not now,
when a dim denizen of darkness
has spread
among the nations of the world,
when the people of the Diaspora
are the most misunderstood.

Teshuva for All

Look in the rear-view mirror.
Stuck in the past and to whom you'll be,
fearful of letting go, of comforts,
of familiarities.

Dig deeper, peel back those
oft hidden layers and years you've
toiled with unwanted warts
of mind and of body.

Teshuva to those times you've cherished
with the breath of what G-d's once created.
Perhaps they are but a few –
not modem, not new.

Return to the month of eternal *Elul*.
A heavy, historic hike of the everlasting,
the traditional, for all of mankind
not just a chosen few.

Ripples

Across my forehead,
across the river's spellbinding stream,
across bank to bank and shore to shore:
Hovers a heavy breath
of perpetual rhythmic waves, a domino-affect
of ripples upon ripples.

Perhaps a pebble pounces and bounces out of sight.
Sea robins and mullet skirt like a flying circus
performing just above the water's surface.
Mother Nature's storm winds blow
with whirlpools just around the river's sharp bend,
and rows and rows of undulating ripples upon ripples.

Somewhere down the stream
at heightened water's speed,
new creeks emerge
out of nothingness.
New unbridled paths forge
where there were no waterways before.

Light and heavy rains blend with
pintsize ripples and colossal ones.
Large *scrub chickens* seek air,
bowfins search for bugs,
monsters of the seas lurk deep,
while bass hide in the chilly caves and
silken seagrasses below.

The Red Sea was parted:
Divided through divine providence.
The Jordan River now
begrudgingly flows,
leisurely goes,
southward into the Dead Sea.

Each *ruach*-like ripple
whispers and endures,
cleanses the murky algae,
returns the waterfowl to their homes.
The sea creatures proceed to their abodes and
tzedakah and humanity to our souls.

Each new year refreshes with *Tashlich*
casting its ills, licking its wounds.
Mistakes become part of the past,
evaporating ripples circle.
Rolling over, vanishing until,
Rosh Hashanah comes again.

My Korban Quest

"I sought your nearness, with all my heart I called you,
and in my going out to meet you I found you coming toward me."
- Israeli poet, Yehudi Levi

No ancient sacrifice
no *binding of Isaac*, in view.
Yes, to the test for a divine mensch, prophet, sage, to ensue.
Yes, to the third Temple rebuilt real soon.

Yes, to the quest for *tzedakah*.
Yes, to all whom sign on.
Yes, to a subsequent soul, good Karma
blanketing all the earth.

Lovingkindness at the forefront,
righteousness to follow.
Then and only then, will the *Mashiach* truly become
the gift instead for me,

for all *tzadiks* whose face of G-d you'll see.
While climbing Jacob's ladder am I,
bridging beyond the holy mountains of Moriah and Sinai,
uncovering *matzahs* for all to share – before they die.

Remember To Turn Off Your Flash

No camera flashes allowed while at Auschwitz
in homage and respect for the dead,
said our tour guide named Luke.
His immense presence there was no fluke
after inheriting this post from his Polish grandmother:
A guide there for many, many years.
His legacy, on this frigid day, he carried
like an eternal burning torch: A *Ner Tamid*.
Unwittingly, my flash went off.
I was frozen.
Anger erupted in his eyes,
glaring, piercing my soul.
He stifled me to the point –
where you see,
no longer did I stand free,
from the camp's
life-changing catastrophe.

That day into the concentration camp
Never again rang like
a theme, an accompanying song,
I could not get out of my head –
Turn off your flash!

His stare and piercing eyes
looking down at me,
put ice in my veins.
They were following me from room to room,
wherever he would go.
I must have butt-clicked the display on the camera,
thought it was off,
as he announced again aloud for everyone to hear –
Turn off your flash!

Early in the morning the day before,
while showering in the nearby hotel
not far from Auschwitz,
my anxiousness had taken hold of me.
Suddenly, a disconcerting dark sound of strange piped-in music
weighed heavily on my burdened soul.

From now on I will remember.
To never, ever again forget and:
Turn off my flash!

If Philosophers Were King

Would not the world be a better place,
if philosophers were king?

Hopefully you've known someone to look up to –
a mentor, a hero, a teacher,
who's uplifted you.
If only they, the *crownless,* were king.*

Someone sent with *ruach.*
not some wizard behind a curtain
but a soul who had seen the face of G-d.
Messengers who have climbed ladders, bridged mighty waters.

We are all given gifts to grasp
well into the heavens.
If only, if only
philosophers were king.

The Philosopher King's Watering Hole

Once while in a college class
in a rush to go fishing early,
my friends anxiously awaited.
Rustling, huddling, outside my professor's door.

It was an expedition to a fishing hole
where the lunkers were abundant.
Sensing my buddies were anxious and obnoxious:
The philosopher, who would be king, cared less.

To this day, I can hear him chiding me
about these *nincompoops* salivating in the hallway.
For he was already in his watering hole –
the sacred classroom, where he was king.

The Stargazer

Venomous Stargazer fish of the sea,
if not handled most carefully,
she will sting her poison and
spritz her spray.
For her luscious taste belies
the dangers that linger deep below
on the ocean floor.

This tree of knowledge with her fruit bearing gifts.
The kind of fruit
that granted free will,
choice, and *achrayut*.
Doors open and close for both fish and fruit.
Guardedly watch your touch,
cautiously watch what you eat.

Shema – Hear me, oh Israel when Moses declared
to meditate aloud, to focus, for "Miriam's Well" was dry.
G-d heedfully ordered *to draw forth water* from the rock.
Listen meticulously to the words, to the trees,
to the Heaven-sent stars
of our forefathers, or
be stung by the Stargazers.

At-One-Ment with Nature's Gifts

With great anticipation
I look forward to
when the stars align and
when the skies seamlessly blend
into the seas' silky way.
At one with Nature's gifts,
where the dropped silvery bait
can be seen shining vividly,
on the Gulf of Mexico's floor.
The perfect conditions –
fifteen miles out for a
once in a quarter century catch
of an elusive, two-foot red grouper.

Mightily, this old man and the sea,
pulls up and reels in
a poor man's lobster:
Its red color accenting the backdrop,
of the serene, blue waters.
Look at it this way, e pluribus Unum;
where the sky, the fiery looking fish,
the water and me,
are all at-one-ment.

Jump forward to another once in a lifetime day
when I limited out
on two magnificent, lunker, gag groupers
from the bow of the boat!
I paused as we headed back to shore
to observe these two groupers silhouetted in the clouds,
to appear suddenly against the dim sky,
divine faces only exceeded
by Your Heavenly presence.

Smiling Down Upon

"Above the thunder of the mighty waters, more majestic than the breakers of the sea, is Adonai majestic on high." - Psalm 93

Boating was choppy early.
While midday water conditions
veered gloriously bright with an unblemished sky.
Calm and serene was the water's wonderful unanimity,
when we returned
after a long, long,
gratifying day at sea.

Amidst the cascading, emerging, cumulus clouds,
G-d's eyes first appeared to follow from the stern
of our boat: Not unlike a Mona Lisa's stare.
On second glance these clouds sketched
the profile of a huge grouper-looking fish.
Then, blindly transformed this denizen of the deep
into the semblance of a sleek shark.

On third glance my eyes became more focused,
thinking there was no *burning bush* to be found anywhere.
Where were the eyedrops when needed
for all to believe, to better see?
The silhouette emerged from the image of G-d's facsimilied face,
his eyes I envisioned piercing my soul,
his mouth smirking, only his divinity
smiling down upon me.

Author's Notes

"Would I Have Survived" - *Tzadik* is the Hebrew term given for a righteous or just person. *Elijah* is symbolic of bringing the Messiah to come. Biblical accounts state Elijah ascended to Heaven and didn't die (during the messianic age 20 centuries ago). *Elijah* is referring to the prophet, defender, messenger, and welcomed guest at the Passover Seder dinner by virtue of a cup of wine at the table and an opening of the front door.

"Could a Hitler Rise Again?" - In reference to and recognition of Vance Packard's, <u>Nation of Strangers</u> and Robert Putnam's book, <u>Bowling Alone</u>.

"What Being a Jew Means" - *L'dor Vador* is the Hebrew phrase meaning to pass from generation to generation. Specifically, it is the responsibility of passing on and sustaining the Jewish peoples' collective memory, spiritual wisdom, and cultural traditions from generation to generation.

"On Faith" - For your/my sake was the world created phrase from Talmud. See **Tales of the Hasidim Later Masters** by Martin Buber. "I am nothing but dust and ashes." - Genesis. Buber discusses the "two pockets" analogy of Rabbi Simcha Bunim, whereby when a person is too proud and mighty, they should remember "I am but dust and ashes". Conversely, if one is lowly and disheartened, recite "for my sake was the world created." "I will leap, and the net will appear." - Buddha saying about faith.

"On Faith" - *Hovering upon the waters* comes from Genesis 1:2 (in the Old Testament) and is interpreted as a 'great wind' (a Hebrew phrase) with derivation from *Ruach Elohim* - the breath of G-d. Water was before the earth and *G-d was there in the face of the waters, breathing over it. Nefesh* is the Hebrew word for soul.

"Love Inspires" - *Tzedakah(s)* in Hebrew means charity, moral obligation, an act of loving-kindness. The poem "Love Inspires" was provoked by a prose in the Siddur book, Mishkan T'Filah, entitled *Prayer Invites*. "I am my beloved's, and my beloved is mine who browses among the lilies." - Song of Solomon 6:3.

"Rifka's Mezuzah" - *Mezuzahs* are placed in Jewish homes on their doorposts. It contains the prayer called the *Shema* which is Judaism's most important prayer - in remembrance of one G-d. In reverence, Jewish people kiss the *Mezuzah* upon entering the home and as a constant reminder of G-d's presence. Hence, the phrase *coming in and going out.*

"Rifka's Mezuzah" - The *Shema* is an ancient prayer in Deuteronomy affirming that there is one G-d. It is the declaration of the Judaic faith and often the last prayer said before death.

"Checked Your Mezuzah Lately?" - *Checked your mezuzah lately?* Refers to primarily Orthodox Jew's tongue in cheek expression – to make sure/to stay focused during a person's difficult times one should do a quality check – to see if the parchment's ink (inside their mezuzah) was smudged or needed to be replaced. To be a *light unto the nation* refers to the Jewish community being the receiver of the Torah and the Ten Commandments thus morally obligated to share the teachings and utterances, respectively.

"The Shema: A Watchword Prayer" - "If you pray only according to the precise text in the siddur and nothing from your heart your prayer is not complete." - Talmud *Ein od, Ein od* is the Hebrew phrase which refers to G-d being everything, no other, no end.

"Seahorse Stables Shabbat" - *Shabbat* or the Sabbath is honored by Jews to observe the Biblical Seventh Day of Rest to commemorate G-d's resting day after creating the world.

"My Soul"- *Nefesh* in Hebrew means one's soul. *The Burning Palace* is a parable about G-d's palace not unlike the present world in strife, with many injustices, and bloodshed. The Midrash brings to question where is G-d? Who rules, who owns the *palace*?

"The Jewish Way" - *Sechel* in Hebrew means intellect, wit, reason. *Kvelling* in Yiddish means extraordinarily pleased with one's family member.

"Misunderstood" - *Smoked vapor* is used in many contexts, symbolically, abstractly, and metaphorically. Judaically, most often in the Talmud and referenced in Ecclesiastes 1:2 and 12:8. Here it is used in terms of the human condition, life's difficulties, and in helping to discern normative truth. *Talmud* is the holy oral teachings/traditions that expands the written text of the Torah. *Torah* is the first Five Books of Moses - Genesis, Exodus, Leviticus, Numbers, and Deuteronomy. Also known as The Bible, The Holy Scriptures, the Old Testament.

"Misunderstood" - *Refers to *Let My People Go,* Moses said to Pharoah, quoting G-d, to taking the Jews out of slavery then to the land of Israel *to serve and to be responsible to G-d.*

"Teshuva for All" - *Teshuva* meaning in Hebrew, a return or repentance. Historically, it is the sacred 10 days between the Jewish High Holidays of the new year called Rosh Hashanah and the day of atonement, Yom Kippur. Also, referred to as the *Days of Awe.*

"Teshuva for All" - "It is a tree of life for those who hold fast to it, and all its supporters are happy. Its ways are ways of pleasantness, and all its paths are peace. Return us to You, Adonai, and we will return; renew our days as of old." Prayer said after returning the Torah to the Ark and to not abandon its good instruction.

"Ripples" - *Scrub chickens* are gopher tortoises. *Ruach* is referring to the life force in G-d's breath. In Hebrew it symbolizes one's soul. *Tzedakah* is described on the previous page. *Tashlich* is the ceremony performed on the new year Jewish High Holiday of *Rosh*

Hashanah. Literally it means to cast. Throwing pebbles or bread into bodies of water are customary ways to cast off sins/ mistakes of the previous year.

"My Korban Quest" - *Matzah* is the unleavened, glorified cracker symbolizing change, transformation. Represented on the Passover seder plate commemorating Jews fleeing in haste out of Egypt from bondage to freedom. *Mashiach* is the Hebrew word for messiah.

"Remember to Turn Off Your Flash" - *Ner Tamid* is the Hebrew for *eternal light* - a lamp that bums continuously in Jewish synagogues near the ark. Symbolizes the menorah of the ancient Temple and G-d's eternal presence.

"If Philosophers Were King" - *Ruach* is the Hebrew word for the breath of G-d. It is the essence of life's force. Rabbis say, "in that breath the world was created." Thusly, G-d blew into the nostrils of Adam. The word *crownless* refers to a phrase in J.R.R. Tolkien's poem, "All That is Gold Does Not Glitter".

"The Philosopher King's Watering Hole" - *King* is authentically accepted to mean G-d, his kingdom, in biblical references. In societal referencing, patriarchal characteristic attributes here are most noteworthy and kinglike. No disrespect intended.

"The Stargazer" - *Achrayut* is a widely used Hebrew word that means responsibility, accountability. It also can connote an obligation to improve certain situations morally, politically, militarily.

Acknowledgements

Could a Hitler Rise Again? – Poetica Publishing, A Collection of Contemporary Jewish Learning (Fall 2014). Revised

Love Inspires – Wider Perspectives Publishing in a slightly different adaptation, Florida's Forgotten Crackers (January 2021).
Was inspired by a prose in the Siddur book, Mishkan T'Filah entitled *Prayer Invites.*

Rifka's Mezuzah and *Hanukkah of Old* – photographs by Dr. Robyn Spirtas

Rifka Glatz interview which inspired *Rifka's Mezuzah* and *Checked Your Mezuzah Lately?*

About the Author

Neil Spirtas' poetry can be found in the *Roam, Poetica: Contemporary Jewish Writing, Free Expressions, The Soul's Bright Home, The Eclectic Muse: A Poetry Journal and the Current magazines/anthologies, The Huffington Post*'s - <u>To Publish or Not to Be Published? Today's Climate for Poet's Works</u>, and upcoming <u>Decameron Days</u> by the Hampton Roads Artistic Collective. Reader and contributor in T*he Struggle for Liberty* Anthology Collection by Moonstone Press. His debut chapbook (in 2020) was *When Men Cry: Life's Later Voyages,* and *Florida's Forgotten Crackers* (2021) was nominated for the 2022 North American Book Award. Spirtas was a recipient of the SUNSPRA (a state of Fl. school association) Margie Davidson Leading Light Award while at the Manatee Chamber.

He received a master's degree in Community Development from the University of Missouri. At first a pre-journalism student, he only later in life homed in on his latent talents as a writer. He worked as an executive for three universities and the state of Florida in the field of Community/Economic Development and as a career coach. After three decades as a VP, Spirtas retired from the award-winning Manatee Chamber of Commerce in Bradenton, Florida.

www.ingramcontent.com/pod-product-compliance
Lightning Source LLC
LaVergne TN
LVHW051819080426
835513LV00017B/2012